Praise for
When Action Follows Heart

"Kindness, gratitude, and service have real power to transform our lives, which is why this little inspiring book can have such a huge impact. Susan Spencer gives us a year's worth of ideas for how to both change the lives of those around us and become our better selves." — **Arianna Huffington,** founder of *The Huffington Post* and Founder/CEO of Thrive Global

"We all want to be kinder—and we've all used the excuse that we don't know where to start. Well, the staff of *Woman's Day* has blown that excuse out of the water. You may not use every idea in *When Action Follows Heart,* but even doing a few of them will change your life—and the lives of others." — **Dave Ramsey,** nationally syndicated radio talk show host and *New York Times* best-selling author

"I love this book! The ideas suggested are the very things that make a life—and I'm giddy to actually go do them. My vibe has been raised and that's just the beginning of the good this book will do in your life." — **Mike Dooley,** *New York Times* best-selling author of *From Deep Space with Love* and *Playing the Matrix*

"When you give, you grow. This book will help you shed light on the immense capacity for good in the people around us." — **Mehmet Oz, M.D.,** Emmy award-winning host, *The Dr. Oz Show* and author of *Food Can Fix It*

"Kindfulness is the new mindfulness! This beautiful book helps you to live a life you love by being a loving presence in other people's lives." — **Robert Holden,** author of *Life Loves You* and *Holy Shift!*

"This inspiring collection is like a call to kindness. If you feel the impulse to do good in the world, the ideas in this book will quickly set you on the right path. You might find yourself addicted!" — **Joan Lunden,** journalist, advocate, and *New York Times* best-selling author

"Over the years, I've learned that kindness and generosity create gratitude. And grateful people are some of the most attractive people on the planet! If you're looking for a way to get your eyes off yourself and start making a difference in the world around you, *When Action Follows Heart* has to be on your must-read list." — **Rachel Cruze,** *New York Times* best-selling author of *Love Your Life, Not Theirs*

Hay House Titles of Related Interest

When
Action
Follows
Heart

365 Ways to Share Kindness

Susan Spencer
Editor-in-Chief, Woman'sDay

HAY HOUSE, INC.
Carlsbad, California • New York City
London • Sydney • Johannesburg
Vancouver • New Delhi

Published and distributed in the United States by: Hay House, Inc.: www
.hayhouse.com® · **Published and distributed in Australia by:** Hay House
Australia Pty. Ltd.: www.hayhouse.com.au · **Published and distributed
in the United Kingdom by**: Hay House UK, Ltd.: www.hayhouse.co.uk ·
Distributed in Canada by: Raincoast Books: www.raincoast.com · **Published in India by:** Hay House Publishers India: www.hayhouse.co.in

Cover design and Interior design: Jenny Richards
Front-cover and Interior illustrations: Jutta Kuss

Cataloging-in-Publication Data is on file at the Library of Congress

Hardcover ISBN: 978-1-4019-5552-6

10 9 8 7 6 5 4 3 2 1
1st edition, April 2018
Printed in the United States of America

SUSTAINABLE
FORESTRY
INITIATIVE
Certified Chain of Custody
Promoting Sustainable Forestry
www.sfiprogram.org
SFI-01268
SFI label applies to the text stock

Introduction

A Little Book of Optimism

One of my favorite columns in Woman's Day is the Kindness Project. The idea behind it is very simple: we showcase our readers' kind acts toward others. The column is one of the most popular in the magazine, and we always have a steady stream of submissions from people eager to share their good deeds.

As the idea of turning the column into a book took shape, I began to gather more stories and to ask others how they had witnessed and experienced kindness. I found myself totally immersed in generosity, and it had a wonderful effect. I was more attuned to kindness around me and noticed kind acts almost every day: a man helping an elderly stranger into a seat on a bus, a bunch of zinnias from a community garden appearing on a sick neighbor's doorstep. I was even inspired to kindness myself--I'm the bad driver who bumped (gently!) a woman's fender and left a gift card on her windshield.

I came to realize that this book isn't just about kindness. It's about the instinct to reach out to others to connect and the warmth we feel when we genuinely help someone. It's about forgiveness, civility, mercy, and love. A single act of kindness, whether to a friend or a stranger, can become a spool of generosity that unwinds and touches the lives of so many.

It's my hope that one—or maybe more—of the ideas, reader stories, and quotations in this book will lead you to action. Start by turning to today's date, or flip to any page for random inspiration. Kindness is exactly what we need in our fractured world right now—it provides the simplest path to healing. Let's all begin.

January 1

Make a New Year's resolution to mail a card to a different friend, relative, or acquaintance every week. You never know what each day may bring, and your card could be the one thing that gives them a sign of hope or feeling of love.

January 2

Each week, starting in January, put $1 in a Christmas jar. Two weeks before Christmas, you'll have $50. Pick up a $50 gift certificate from a grocery store and give it anonymously to a family who can't afford food for the holidays.

January 3

Leave a stack of quarters on an arcade game or a laundromat washing machine.

January 4

Moving? Tape a list with the names and numbers of local plumbers, electricians, and dry cleaners, along with other helpful information, on a kitchen cabinet for the people who are coming in.

January 5

Give a lottery ticket to a stranger on the street.

January 6

Bring a little levity when visiting a friend in the hospital: dress up as the Easter Bunny or Batman, or another costumed character.

January 7

Play an instrument? Volunteer to perform at a local senior center. Get those toes tapping!

January 8

Keep a bag in your car designated for food pantry donations so you never forget to pick up canned goods when you shop.

January 9

If you're out for a meal and have some extra cash, choose another table and pay for their dinner.

January 10

"One day I unknowingly dropped my wallet—which basically contained my whole life—on the subway. A random woman picked it up, got off the subway at the next stop (not hers), and gave it to a police officer, who delivered it to my doorstep. It was like something out of a storybook! The cop gave me her number and I called and offered to send her money as a thank you. But, like a true Good Samaritan, she wouldn't give me her mailing address."

January 11

"Kindness is a language the dumb can speak and the deaf can hear and understand."

— Christian Nestell Bovee

January 12

Do double duty: on your next trip to the drugstore, buy two of everything on your list (use coupons!) and give the extras to a local women's shelter.

January 13

Offer to help a friend meet a goal, whether it's running a 5K or losing 10 pounds. This might mean checking in via text once a day, calling once a week, or having your buddy e-mail you her progress—whatever is most helpful.

January 14

When a friend or loved one passes away, collect photos or stories about that person and share them with her family. They will appreciate keeping cherished memories alive.

January 15

The next time a friend makes a delicious meal, ask for the recipe. She'll be flattered—and you'll add a great new dish to your repertoire.

January 16

Collect extra cell phone chargers and donate them to a local hospital. Then people visiting loved ones can focus on the patient, not on battery life.

January 17

"After my friend Jan was diagnosed with stage-four cancer, I would occasionally prepare meals for her. Then came a reverse act of kindness: Jan was an accomplished quilter, and when she heard I was about to welcome a great-granddaughter, she made a quilt for me to give to the baby. I was so delighted. This was the last quilt she ever made before she passed."

January 18

Sign up to receive a poem a day at Poets.org and share it with friends who appreciate words.

January 19

At the gym, put free weights, mats, resistance bands, kettlebells, and any other equipment back where you found it once you are finished. And if you're feeling extra generous, wipe them off with a sanitizing cloth.

January 20

"At the doctor's office recently, I watched a woman being turned away because she didn't have her co-pay. As she left in tears, I quickly paid it, then found her before she could leave and let her know it was taken care of."

January 21

"After hearing about kids who lost their possessions in a fire, we collected more than 1,000 stuffed animals and then gave them to our local fire department. Now when the firefighters respond to a fire, they can give the kids something to hold on to."

January 22

Name a star after someone at Star Registry.com.

January 23

"While I was in line to buy movie tickets, I overheard a woman with three children wondering if she could also afford popcorn. So on the spur of the moment, I paid for their tickets. Seeing how happy the children were—and hearing their thanks—made my day."

January 24

Sometimes a simple hug is worth a thousand kind words.

January 25

When you're cleaning snow and ice off your car in a parking lot, do the next car over as well.

January 26

A kind reminder on a roadside sign: "You're never too important to be nice to people."

January 27

"I receive a lot of coupons for local restaurants and since there are always extras, my husband and I enjoy picking out people to share the savings with when we go out to eat. After they learn they'll get an extra $5 or $10 off their meal, their surprise and gratitude make us wish we had a coupon to give to every table!"

January 28

Throw a party for a friend who's caring for an elderly parent or sick child. Caregivers need support too.

January 29

Surprise your colleagues by bringing a batch of homemade snacks to work.

January 30

Leave a love note on your spouse's pillow with a few chocolates.

January 31

"We live in Michigan, where winters are very cold. My son, now 11, told me he wanted to collect blankets for the homeless. His goal was 200 blankets, but he collected over 400 that year. Last year his goal was 400, and he got 906. We passed them out in the park and took some to the mission. This year his goal is 800, and I can't wait to see how many he gets. His heart for the homeless is such a blessing."

February 1

Redecorate an old recipe box with washi tape, fill it with a few favorite recipes, and give it to a friend who loves to cook.

February 2

Slip an envelope containing a tea bag into a friend's purse with a note inviting her to take some relaxing time for herself.

February 3

"I held the door open for two elderly ladies at the local bakery. As I started to enter after them, they stopped me and said, 'Your mother did a good job with you.' I smiled and said, 'Yes, she did.'"

February 4

When you're done with a great book, give it to a friend you think would enjoy it.

February 5

Buy coloring books and crayons and donate them to your local police department. When the police are called to a home where there are children, one officer can engage the kids while the other handles the situation.

February 6

"As I stood in line at a department store recently, I noticed that the person in front of me had a lot of purchases, so I offered to share my savings pass with her. She was so happy to shave money off her bill, and I was glad to help."

February 7

Smile at an unsmiling person. It doesn't take long for them to return it!

February 8

Give blood on a regular basis. Donating is free, and your gift can be—literally—lifesaving.

February 9

"I teach writing classes at senior centers. My students' stories are so great, and I have helped a number of them get their essays published. Then they can see their writing in book form. We have a blast!"

February 10

When a friend passes away, make a note in your calendar. On the anniversary, send a thinking-of-you card to her family. It means so much to know a loved one is still being remembered.

February 11

Take a sick friend to a doctor's appointment or treatment so she doesn't have to worry about transportation.

February 12

Make a "blessing bag": fill a large Ziploc bag with tissues, wet wipes, trial-size toiletries, socks, and a few dollars, and keep several on hand to distribute to homeless people you encounter.

February 13

Use an online community swap group to post pictures of found items—stray mittens, a child's stuffed animal—so their rightful owners can claim them.

February 14

Send a valentine to a friend who isn't in a relationship to help take the sting out of this couples-focused day.

February 15

"I love to knit ruffled scarves. When I wear them, I get lots of compliments. Needless to say, I rarely come home with a scarf. Giving them away randomly is a great joy to me and a surprising delight to the recipient."

February 16

Stock your car trunk with plastic flat-ware packets and cans of food with pull tabs. When you see a person with a "hungry" sign, give them a can of food that they can enjoy on the spot.

February 17

If someone is short a few dollars at the store, make up the difference.

February 18

"Wherever there is a human being, there is an opportunity for a kindness."

— Seneca

February 19

Write your favorite elementary school teacher a thank-you note relating the most important lesson you learned from her.

February 20

"Someone once said, 'Don't ever hesitate to give a compliment.' I try to give one every day, and I'm often rewarded with a smile."

February 21

Yield an open parking space to the other person vying for it.

February 22

If someone's doing great work, send her boss an e-mail or note to sing her praises.

February 23

"While browsing in a local thrift shop, I noticed a woman wearing an apron from a nearby store. She was shopping on her break. She admired a dress and said she'd have to come back when she had the money. Knowing the dress would be snapped up, I bought it for her after she left and took it to the store where she worked. The huge smile I received was the only thanks I needed!"

February 24

Secretly decorate a friend's front door with streamers and balloons in honor of her birthday. She'll come home to an instant party!

February 25

Create a joyful playlist for a friend going through a rough patch.

February 26

Tell a parent they're doing a good job.
(They probably rarely hear that!)

February 27

"I always make it a point to tell a supervisor or manager how pleased I am when a salesperson gives me helpful and cheerful service. Often the response is, 'We usually hear the negative, so we appreciate you taking time for the positive.'"

February 28

Park carefully—between the lines—so you won't prevent someone from pulling in comfortably next to you.

February 29

Have a sweet-tempered pup? Have them certified as a therapy dog and bring them to nursing homes and schools to spread a little happiness.

March 1

Every so often, write and mail a quick, cheery note to an elderly friend or neighbor.

March 2

When you reach for a stick of gum, a mint, or a candy in your bag, offer one to everyone around you.

March 3

"Whenever I see someone taking a family photo, I offer to snap the shot so everyone can be included in the moment. You never know—that photo could be featured on their holiday card that year or become a treasured memento. And folks almost always offer to return the favor!"

March 4

Share the savings! If you have extra coupons you're not using at the register, give them to the people in line behind you.

March 5

"I always keep free sample bags of dog food from the vet's office or Ziploc bags full of dog food in our car. When I am driving through town and see a homeless person on a corner with a dog, I give them a bag of dog food. My family and I are huge animal lovers and it feels good to know that we are helping in a little way."

March 6

When a new family moves into the neighborhood, use chalk to leave welcome messages on the sidewalk in front of their home.

March 7

After a hospital stay, make cookies for the nurses and support staff, wrap them individually, and enclose little thank-you notes—these hardworking folks deserve special recognition.

March 8

"When a friend had her second baby, I e-mailed several of her other friends and invited them to sign up on Meal Train.com to bring her family a home-cooked dinner. My friend didn't have to think about food for a couple of weeks. She could spend that precious time focusing on her new bundle of joy (or catching up on sleep!)."

March 9

When you see stray shopping carts outside a supermarket, take a few minutes to bring them back into the store.

March 10

Create a reward system for kindness in your house. Put a chart on the refrigerator and add a sticker every time someone in the family does something nice. When the chart's full, go out for a family treat (hello, ice cream!).

March 11

"Moving to a new neighborhood can be lonely, especially for women who've left behind their former social network. I buy a bouquet of flowers and drop by a new neighbor's house to introduce myself. I give them my phone number and chat about the town, stores, churches, and schools, and ask if they need referrals. I've made some good friends this way."

March 12

Raise a kind kid by encouraging her to model generosity. She might want to share a picture she drew, read a book to a younger student, or invite a new friend over to play.

March 13

Reap what you sow: anonymously leave baking supplies for a co-worker who loves to bring cookies and confections to the office.

March 14

"When my mom turned 80, my parents threw two big birthday parties and turned them into fund-raisers. One was for flood victims in Nepal and the other was for football lights at the club where my dad helps manage a local team. They didn't want presents. This was an opportunity to give back."

March 15

"Be the living expression of God's kindness: kindness in your face, kindness in your eyes, kindness in your smile."

— Mother Teresa

March 16

Give a box of old clothing—hats, boas, capes, scarves, jackets, dresses—to a young child who loves to play dress up. The sparklier, the better!

March 17

On Saint Patrick's Day, leave a little gift from the leprechauns for a neighbor's kids.

March 18

"When my husband died, our family let friends know that performing a random act of kindness would be a wonderful way to honor him. Knowing people were doing good deeds on his behalf has helped us cope."

March 19

Put chocolate chip cookies in your mailbox with a note thanking the postal carrier.

March 20

On the first day of spring, leave a basket full of bulbs on a neighbor's doorstep with a note offering to plant them.

Spring for you

March 21

Join the Kindness Rocks Project (the kindnessrocksproject.com) and paint a small stone with an inspiring message. Leave it in a public place for someone to find.

March 22

"For a friend who was having a baby, I collected 6-by-6-inch squares of cloth that represented wishes for the future. Then I sewed them together into a handmade patchwork blanket. She loved it!"

March 23

Dogs and cats need kindness too! Take your family to visit a local animal shelter. Even if you can't take a pet home, you can play with them for an hour.

March 24

Offer to babysit for free for a frazzled mom or dad, or take over their shift as the carpool parent.

March 25

One small kind gesture could literally save a life: register to become a bone marrow donor at BeTheMatch.org.

March 26

Attach balloons and an "It's a Girl!" or "It's a Boy!" sign to a new mom's mailbox. This sweet gesture will invite neighbors to come by with gifts and say congratulations.

March 27

Pet sit for someone who is going away on vacation.

March 28

Make a list of the people you are closest to and mark a calendar (online or on paper) with their birthdays and wedding anniversaries. Then set a digital calendar reminder one week in advance for each occasion and mail a handwritten note.

March 29

"I am connected on Facebook with people from all over the world, some of whom I've never met. One such woman sent me a private, unsolicited message that simply said, 'You're beautiful.' I replied, 'Thank you. Such a sweet message.' She wrote, 'I don't know you personally, but I see your posts. I know you'll succeed in whatever you do. God has honored his promises to you.' It was so unexpectedly kind and thoughtful."

March 30

Carry a battery charger in your trunk to help people whose cars have stalled.

March 31

Save boxes from packages that you get in the mail and give them to a friend who is moving.

April 1

Visit MealsOnWheelsAmerica.org to find out how to deliver food to those in need in your community.

April 2

Text or e-mail a friend a link to an article with a note that says: "I thought about you when I saw this."

April 3

See if your small business can give back in some way. A dry cleaners in Portland, Oregon, posts a sign on its door that says: "If you are unemployed and need an outfit cleaned for an interview, we will clean it for free."

April 4

Surprise your spouse on a weekend morning with breakfast in bed. Ask your children to help you make the meal, and they can be part of the big reveal too.

April 5

Support your local businesses! If you had a great meal at a restaurant, take the time to write a positive review on Yelp.com. Or if you were treated by a wonderful doctor, give that physician a thumbs-up on Vitals.com. If a land-scaping service did a great job with your yard, give the company a positive review on AngiesList.com.

April 6

Instead of selling old items or clothing at a garage sale or on Craigslist, donate them to a local shelter or the Salvation Army. Or you can give them to others via Freecycle.org.

April 7

Buy extra umbrellas and keep them in your car. When you see someone caught in a downpour, hand one over.

April 8

Say you're sorry to someone whose feelings you hurt (whether accidentally or intentionally). Be the bigger person.

April 9

"While in line to buy lunch, I met a hardworking young man saving for college. When I said I wanted to help him put away a few more dollars by paying for his meal, he smiled at me from the inside out. His reaction felt like the real gift."

April 10

Make a "coupon" for a casserole and give it to a friend or neighbor to redeem whenever she could use a night off from cooking.

April 11

Build a mini-library on a street corner in your neighborhood to encourage literacy and foster community. Neighbors can take out books and replace them with others. Go to LittleFreeLibrary .org for ideas.

April 12

When you know that a friend has something important or stressful coming up—like a job interview or a breakup—send her a text that simply says, "Thinking of you." Then check in with her later.

April 13

"My grandmother is 98 and in assisted living, mentally all there but with numerous physical issues. My mother and my three aunts, who visit her regularly, have been encouraging her to share memories from her childhood, then taking the time to write down what she says. It clearly helps her to relate seemingly mundane recollections about things like her childhood cat and its unintentional destruction of her mother's prized lampshade."

April 14

Just say hello. Add a smile and you've doubled your kindness quotient for the day.

April 15

Wash a friend's car. Think of it as extra exercise!

April 16

Leave a basket of tennis balls at a dog-friendly beach or park with a sign that says, "For your pup to enjoy."

April 17

"Be a rainbow in somebody else's cloud."

— Maya Angelou

April 18

Practice kindness in conversation: actively listen to a friend who is talking, and ask follow-up questions to show you're engaged.

April 19

Courtesy counts: help an elderly person up a staircase.

April 20

Don't use customer-service represen-
tatives solely as a sounding board
for complaints. Call to thank them
for particularly good service. (They'll
probably be shocked!)

April 21

"When a small restaurant opened in my neighborhood in a location where past businesses had struggled, I not only began patronizing it regularly but also posted its menu on community social media sites along with praise for the food and the owner's dedication. Others soon joined in giving accolades, and now, over a year later, the restaurant is going strong."

April 22

Be kind to the earth! Turn off the tap while you brush your teeth, switch to paperless billing, recycle, use energy-efficient light bulbs, use a refillable water bottle, and bring cloth bags to the supermarket.

April 23

Send a book of poems or a devotional to a grieving friend.

April 24

The simplest act of kindness is to say,
"Thank you."

April 25

"I quietly paid for a friend in my women's group to go on a church retreat. She was elderly and on a fixed income and couldn't afford it. I loved seeing how happy she was when she found out she could go."

April 26

If you see someone with a stroller near a staircase and there's no elevator in sight, help her up or down the stairs.

April 27

If you receive someone else's mail by mistake, hand-deliver it to the person's house.

April 28

Let the person in line behind you at the supermarket—the one who has two items to your massive cartload—jump ahead of you.

April 29

Make a bunch of paper airplanes with your child. Then hand them out to other kids at your local park.

April 30

Do yourself a kindness: forgive yourself for a past mistake that's been nagging at you.

May 1

Take the time to learn the name of someone who regularly helps you out—whether it's a security guard, a doorman, or a cashier at your grocery store. Greet them by name.

May 2

If there is a senior citizen in your neighborhood who can't drive, offer to chauffeur her once a week to a hair salon, the mall, or a restaurant.

May 3

Share your skills! If you're a good artist, show a little one how to draw something. Tech savvy? Help someone figure out her computer or phone.

May 4

Greet the person next to you in the elevator.

May 5

"During my daughter's hospitalization, we spent many days at her bedside. The best care package we received arrived on Cinco de Mayo, when a friend sent us margarita mix, fun cups, straws, and maracas."

May 6

As your family outgrows clothes, wash them and place them in a designated laundry hamper. Every time it's full, arrange for a donation pickup at VVApickup.org.

May 7

Write a glowing recommendation for a current or past co-worker on LinkedIn to help that person get ahead in the workplace.

May 8

"A home not far from me has a particularly lovely garden. One day when I was walking by, I saw this (laminated!) note left by a passerby: 'Your flowers are beautiful! Thank you for bringing a bit more cheer to the world.'"

May 9

Compliment three different friends on social media, telling them what great people they are.

May 10

Go for a walk with a group of friends at a local park and pick up litter along the way.

May 11

Read magazines on a plane? Don't dump them when you're done—offer them to the flight attendants for their reading pleasure.

May 12

"I expect to pass through this world but once. Any good therefore that I can do, or any kindness that I can show to any fellow creature, let me do it now. Let me not defer or neglect it, for I shall not pass this way again."

— Quaker saying

May 13

On Mother's Day, think about someone who has lost a parent. Invite her out to lunch—you'll be either an emotional support on a tough day or a welcome distraction.

May 14

Leave your phone in your pocket or purse when you're talking to other people face-to-face. Give them all your attention.

May 15

Send your favorite college student a care package full of sweet treats, salty snacks, and caffeine. The next time she pulls an all-nighter, you'll be a hero!

May 16

Rescue old pictures from photo albums, where they are probably fading away. Scan them and e-mail them to the friends or family who are in the shots with a memory of that moment.

May 17

"After my dad passed away, my sister and I were cleaning out his house. A neighbor came by with hot sandwiches, homemade slaw, and dessert because she wanted to make this sad job a little easier."

May 18

Buy a bunch of balloons and hand them out to kids (and adults!) at a local playground.

May 19

Treat your best friend to dinner and a movie for no reason other than to celebrate your friendship.

May 20

Before you make an assumption about someone, give the person the benefit of the doubt and have a conversation about whatever is bothering you. When you're patient and calm and you give someone the chance to explain herself, you may feel less angry—and possibly even realize that you misunderstood.

May 21

Leave a bouquet of flowers at a friend's doorstep, ring the doorbell, and then run like crazy.

May 22

Think about people who may be bringing too much negativity into your life and find the courage to amicably separate yourself. This might mean no longer following them on social media or spending less time with them. Life is short. Be with people who support you and fill you with joy.

May 23

Send inspirational cards to children battling cancer at a local hospital. Put in stickers, temporary tattoos, and coloring pages to help make their mail even more special.

May 24

Join the website Nextdoor.com so you can share and receive important information with your neighbors. You can post about crimes or suspicious activities, potholes, car accidents and traffic, lost pets or items, block parties, local events, and more topics that can help keep others safe and build community.

May 25

Every time you buy a new piece of clothing, follow the "one in, one out" rule: go
through your closet and pull out something that you haven't worn in a while
and donate it to a women's shelter.

May 26

Put some extra change into a random parking meter.

May 27

Have leftover flower arrangements from a wedding or other event? Break them down into bouquets and deliver them to a local senior center.

May 28

Remember your manners! Always say please when making a request. This small gesture can make a big difference.

May 29

Leave a sticky note with an empower-
ing message ("You're beautiful!") on
the mirror in a public restroom.

May 30

"The traffic where I live can be incredibly frustrating. I've found that just smiling at my fellow drivers—even if I actually feel like screaming—is a form of kindness for myself and others."

May 31

Be a caring adult role model for a child who may be struggling by joining Big Brothers Big Sisters of America (bbbs.org).

June 1

Bring extra bags to the supermarket to share with people who've forgotten to bring their own.

June 2

Place a disposable cooler filled with chilled water bottles at the end of a walking trail.

June 3

"My husband and I were in line at a little doughnut shop behind an adorable brother and sister, maybe eight and ten years old. When they got to the front, they were struggling to count out the change to pay for their doughnuts. Seeing them trying to get the right amount of coins reminded me what it was like to be a kid again. I asked the server to add their doughnuts to our order. The eight-year-old swung around and said, 'Really? Thank you, thank you, thank you!,' and gave me a big hug."

June 4

Surprise newlyweds coming back from their honeymoon to an empty fridge with a basket of "welcome home" goodies.

June 5

When a handyman or worker comes to your house, offer up a glass of ice water and a snack.

June 6

Hello, cupid! Set up two people you think would make a great romantic match.

June 7

Offer your couch or spare room to a friend who is visiting your area so she doesn't have to spend money on a hotel room.

June 8

Go ahead, brag! Let the valedictorians, prom queens, personal-best achievers, or the newly promoted in your life know you're busting with pride by spreading the news of their success wherever you go.

June 9

"I'm training for a half marathon. One day on a particularly hard run, a fellow female runner smiled as I passed by and shouted, 'Great work! Keep going!' Ever since, I offer the same sentiments to other runners. It feels really good to empower others and share the joy of running."

June 10

Print out a quotation or a song lyric that a friend loves, put it in a frame, and give it to her as a surprise gift.

June 11

Plant a tree with your family.

June 12

When you're checking on a loved one at the hospital or rehab center, ask the nurses if there's a patient who could use some company and pay them a quick visit before you go.

June 13

Develop an organizational system for your e-mails so you don't forget to respond to others. Star e-mails or archive them in a designated folder if you don't have time to reply right away, or set a reminder in your smartphone's calendar.

★ ★

June 14

Offer to be the official photographer at a birthday party, reunion, anniversary, or family vacation. Sometimes people are too busy enjoying themselves or hosting to record the event.

June 15

"One of my neighbors hosts a s'mores night in their driveway every Sunday and invites the neighborhood to come over and join the fun."

June 16

"The only justification we have for looking down on someone is that we're going to stop and pick them up."

— Jesse Jackson

June 17

Turn a family trip into a volunteer vacation. VolunteerWorld.com can help you find a destination that combines good deeds and family fun.

June 18

"My grandchildren set up a lemonade stand and donated what they earned to the Humane Society. They own three puppies and two cats, so this cause is dear to their hearts. They raised $120 in two hours due to the generosity of our neighbors, who stopped by for lemonade and complimentary chocolate chip cookies!"

June 19

Organize an end-of-year lunch for the teachers in your local school to recognize their hard work.

June 20

Volunteer to use your photography skills at a local shelter to take pictures of the dogs or cats. A great picture will make the animal more adoptable.

June 21

Buy a girlfriend a massage or a mani-pedi when she's had a tough week. Better yet, go together!

June 22

If you know someone who is having a hard time, text her a pun or a joke.

June 23

Join a mentorship program at your workplace and help a newbie learn the ropes.

June 24

Forgive someone a debt and never bring it up again.

June 25

If you know a person in your community who is doing good deeds, call a local TV or newspaper reporter to share her story with a wider audience.

June 26

At the end of the school year, encourage your child to write notes or draw pictures for the people who touched her life that year—her teacher, bus driver, principal, or lunch aide.

June 27

"Coming up from the subway into a sudden downpour, I saw a woman huddled in a doorway with no umbrella, so I asked her to join me under mine. I walked her to her destination, which happened to be only two doors down from where I was going."

June 28

Instead of a fancy pen or cash, give a newly minted college grad help with her résumé or interview skills.

June 29

"A young widow with two kids moved next door to my father, and he overheard her telling her son she didn't have time to hang up their basketball hoop right away. That night, after dark, Dad went over and installed it. He hadn't even learned their names yet."

June 30

Be a moving angel and give a friend a few hours of your time to help unpack boxes.

July 1

Set up a sign that says "Stop and chat!" and a couple of chairs on your street corner or in your local park for anyone who might want to take a break on a busy day.

July 2

Weed a neighbor's front or backyard.

July 3

Designate a Crazy Food Day: let your family eat pizza for breakfast, pancakes for dinner, and ice cream anytime.

July 4

When a friend has a baby, bring over dinner—plus a few more meals for the freezer.

July 5

When you're traveling on a crowded subway, train, or bus, be on the lookout for a pregnant, elderly, or disabled person who may need your seat more than you do.

July 6

Make it a rule to never pass a children's lemonade stand without stopping to buy a cup.

July 7

Next time you're on social media, reach out to an old acquaintance and share a positive experience or characteristic you still remember about her years later.

July 8

If a friend has food stuck in her teeth, tell her. She'll appreciate it!

July 9

If you know someone who always listens to the same radio station during her commute, call the station and dedicate a song to her.

July 10

Go to the playground with bottles of bubbles, large pieces of chalk, and stickers, and leave them in a central location for kids to help themselves.

July 11

"Human kindness has never weakened the stamina or softened the fiber of a free people. A nation does not have to be cruel in order to be tough."

— Franklin Delano Roosevelt

July 12

"Every morning on my commute to work, I compliment a woman I don't know. Maybe I'll tell her she has a cute purse or a nice smile—whatever is genuine in the moment. It doesn't cost a cent, and I can see that it makes whoever I talk to feel good."

July 13

Donate gently used children's books to your local library or pediatrician's office.

July 14

When a friend seems overwhelmed, offer to take her car for a wash and oil change, then fill up the gas tank too.

July 15

Don't toss old bread—break it into small pieces and feed the birds in your back-yard. Bring grapes or wilted lettuce to the ducks at a nearby pond.

July 16

"I get coffee at the same place every morning. One day I walked in to find the woman behind the counter on the verge of tears from being hassled by a rude customer. I went home and wrote her a note that told her how much I appreciate her and brought it back the next day."

July 17

Why limit a birthday to just one day?
For the week leading up to the date,
leave out notes, coupons, or small gifts
for the person turning a year older.

July 18

When you're finished reading a news-paper or magazine on a bus or train, leave it in the seat pocket so the next person who boards can read it for free.

July 19

Tell your husband not to make any plans on a certain day and then schedule a "dudes' date" for him with a few of his best friends at a local bowling alley, bar, or restaurant.

July 20

Don't let distance keep you from treating a friend! If you know someone who's celebrating a birthday or promotion, send her money via Venmo to buy coffee or lunch for herself.

July 21

Instead of birthday gifts, ask friends to give you or your child books and paja-mas to donate to a local shelter.

July 22

If you see a child go out of his way to help another kid or make her feel welcome, share this kindness with his parents.

July 23

"Every time my mom shops at a store like Target or Michaels—which have bins of inexpensive monogrammed stationery and notepads near the checkout lines—she looks for cute gift items with family members' initials to give them as 'happys' the next time she sees them."

★ ★

July 24

Take a pause before venting on social media and reconsider posting a negative comment. Challenge yourself to posting only positive or complimentary comments online for one week.

July 25

Hold the door for a person with a walker or wheelchair.

July 26

Take photos of your friends and family. Send them the best shots and compliment them on how cute they are.

July 27

Donate gently used work clothes to Dress for Success.

July 28

Help elderly folks remove their luggage from the baggage claim carousel—or give them a hand lifting their bags into the overhead bin.

July 29

"When a mom in our neighborhood passed away this year, people in our community volunteered to make or deliver dinner every night for the first couple of months so her husband didn't have to worry about planning meals for himself and their two young children."

July 30

Leave the restroom cleaner than it was when you found it.

July 31

"A tree fell on my friend's neighbor's house, so she and her husband went over with their chainsaw and helped cut it up into logs. They turned something scary into a fun log-chopping community gathering."

August 1

"Kindness is noticing a problem and fixing it immediately. After I had a baby, a visiting friend saw I was worried about whether the noise in our house was disturbing his sleep. She took charge and ordered me a sound machine. It arrived the next day."

August 2

Grab some slips of paper and on each one, write down something you love about a friend or loved one. Roll them up and put them in a jar. Then give the jar to your friend with instructions to read one every Monday morning for a start-of-the-week pick-me-up.

August 3

"Without judgment or comment, a total stranger at the grocery store loaded my groceries into my car while my son was shrieking and throwing a tantrum. Then she simply continued on her way."

August 4

Help out the summer-weary moms in your neighborhood by creating an obstacle course in your backyard with cones, Hula-Hoops, jump ropes, and whatever else you can find. Call it the Summer Olympics and invite all the kids to join.

August 5

"I try to compliment people when I'm out and about. I feel like the people who talk to me randomly do it because they want to say something rude about me or my parenting style. So I try to be the kind of person who does the exact opposite."

August 6

Don't wait for your child's teacher to request supplies. On the first day of school, send your kid in with a bag of tissues, antibacterial wipes, and paper towels.

August 7

"My husband and I enjoy playing Skee-Ball on our seaside vacations. When we're done, we find a family with kids and, after the parents say it's okay, we give them our winning tickets. It warms our hearts to see them scoot off to the prize booth!"

August 8

Start a cookie-of-the-month club: experiment with a new recipe once a month and share the results with friends and neighbors.

August 9

"I was on a subway train that got stuck for 45 minutes. A young man started having a panic attack. A woman noticed his symptoms, got up, and started to try to calm him down. She sat with him on the floor, helping him breathe. As people noticed what she was doing, the dynamic changed—a man offered me his seat, and strangers started talking to one another. It was wonderful to see what one act of kindness inspired."

August 10

Tip generously if you can. A few extra bucks here and there can really help a person working for an hourly rate.

August 11

"Once when I was out for a walk, I saw a woman struggling to parallel park her car, so I asked if I could help, and got in the car and did it for her."

August 12

"Three things in human life are important. The first is to be kind. The second is to be kind. And the third is to be kind."

— Henry James

August 13

Call your parents and your grandparents regularly.

August 14

To make a friend's birthday even sweeter, organize her friends and family to each write what they love about her (including memories and stories that will make her smile) and compile the contributions into a big list.

August 15

Get into the habit of asking yourself, *How can I help?* and you'll find all kinds of ways to assist others during the course of your day.

August 16

"I've helped several friends declutter. They love the help because it's so much easier to do with another person. And it's fun for me because it's not my own stuff!"

August 17

If you're shopping with a gift card and have a few dollars left on it, pass it back to the person behind you so they can get a small discount on their purchase.

August 18

"After a family vacation, I made my parents a photo book of all the pictures we took during the trip, with captions noting where we were and what we were doing. It was a small way to show my parents I appreciated the time we spent together and to put our memories on paper."

August 19

If you see a car circling a crowded parking lot as you're walking to your own car, let them know you're about to pull out so they can follow you and snag your spot.

★ ★

August 20

"Recently I was hauling my suitcase up a set of stairs at the airport when suddenly my luggage felt 10 pounds lighter. I turned around and saw a woman had picked up my suitcase from the back. Her simple gesture warmed my heart—she was willing to help a stranger, and I didn't even have to ask."

August 21

Visiting a friend with a pet? Instead of a gift for the hostess, bring along a toy or a bone for the real head of the household.

August 22

When you're at a social gathering, make a point of talking to the person who isn't being included in the conversation.

August 23

On social media, compliment a stranger on a particularly fun post.

August 24

When a friend is going through a rough time, organize a bunch of pals to sign a digital card (through GroupCard.com) and e-mail it to her. It's the equivalent of a giant group hug.

August 25

Feeling under the weather and can't make it to that event you planned on? Rather than letting your ticket go unused, offer it to a friend.

August 26

"One day as I was walking into the drugstore, I passed a skinny and desperate young woman who was begging for spare change at the entrance. A few minutes later, the woman walked in holding a shopping basket. A kind, calm man accompanied her around the store, asking her what she needed. He bought her food and medicine, but more importantly, he gave her respect and a chance to be heard."

August 27

Make cards that say, "Don't forget to smile. Hope you have a good day!" and put them on cars around your neighborhood.

August 28

Order a pizza and have it delivered to out-of-town friends dealing with a birth, death, or other major life event.

August 29

Forgive someone who has wronged you in the past. Let it go, move on, and maybe even try to reconnect.

August 30

"An elderly neighbor with an abundant harvest leaves the fresh-picked fruits (and vegetables!) of her labors on her front porch for the entire neighborhood to pick up."

August 31

Help out a sick friend by texting her from the supermarket and asking what she needs.

September 1

Donate arts and crafts supplies to your local library for after-school fun.

September 2

"My brother is a personal trainer at a neighborhood gym. A client he had been working with for three months told him she had to stop the sessions due to unexpected medical bills surrounding a condition that her son had. Knowing that the training was benefiting her physical health and mental well-being and that she needed it now more than ever, my brother offered to continue training her for free. She was so grateful that she ended up referring two new clients to him."

September 3

Make notes in your calendar about big events taking place in your friends' lives. Think beyond the obvious birthday to include occasions like a review at work, kids going off to college, or a dreaded doctor's appointment. When those days come, send that friend an encouraging text.

September 4

"My 10-year-old granddaughter wanted to do something kind for people. A nurse at a local hospital suggested making pillows for patients who have had open-heart surgery. We took up the task, and my granddaughter did a great job. It's a good start to caring about others, and she's learning a new skill at the same time."

September 5

Designate part of your wedding registry for donations to a favorite charity.

September 6

Why wait for Teacher Appreciation Week? Brainstorm ways to be kind to your kids' teachers all year, whether it's sending in a magazine or a homemade treat or bringing breakfast or lunch.

September 7

Call your local school's social worker and offer to anonymously cover the cost of a needy student's school breakfast or lunch, or their books for the year.

September 8

Go to a PTA meeting and propose a kindness-themed event at your child's school. Ask if other parents would be interested in hiring a speaker to give an assembly on the topic.

September 9

"At our school's bookfair each year, we establish a separate collection for a less fortunate school in our district so families can donate books that will go to those children and teachers."

September 10

"A friend just surprised my husband and me with a special dessert for our anniversary. We were at a local spa, and when we came home, a cake was waiting for us with a card. So sweet!"

September 11

Bring a box of doughnuts to your town administrator's office or police or fire station.

September 12

"Being considerate of others will take you and [your children] further in life than any college or professional degree."

— Marian Wright Edelman

September 13

"My 80-year-old mom never goes out for a walk without carrying a plastic bag to collect roadside trash. She loves making the world just a little bit tidier."

September 14

Consider fostering a dog or cat from a local shelter. It eases overcrowding and helps animals acclimate to life in a house.

September 15

"When I was in college, I'd anonymously hide homemade cookies in the carrels to fuel my friends' late-night library study sessions. It was always hilarious listening to them try to guess who was stashing the treats!"

September 16

If you're traveling alone on the train, give up the window seat and sit in the aisle next to a stranger. This makes your seat and the one next to it available for a parent and child to sit together.

September 17

"A boy wanted to buy a toy panda at a store, but his mom couldn't afford it until her next paycheck. The boy wrote on the toy's box: 'Please don't buy this. My mom is going to get it for me on June 15th.' The store workers saw the note and tracked down the boy via Facebook. Then they chipped in to buy it for him."

September 18

"A friend connected me to a grand-mother who needed help taking care of her grandkids after their mother passed away. I sent money to repair the home, buy groceries, and purchase clothing. I also called and e-mailed to give her encouragement. We didn't meet until a year later, because I didn't want her to feel obligated to have any kind of relationship just because I was helping her. I feel like helping someone out, without expecting anything in return, includes not needing to be thanked."

September 19

"In Des Moines, on Free Art Friday, local artists leave artwork in random places for people to find. When I put out one of my photographs, I include an inspiring message to the recipient. I've had quite a few people contact me and say that it made their day!"

September 20

Make a kid giggle by tucking a piece of paper with a sweet note inside the sandwich in her lunch box.

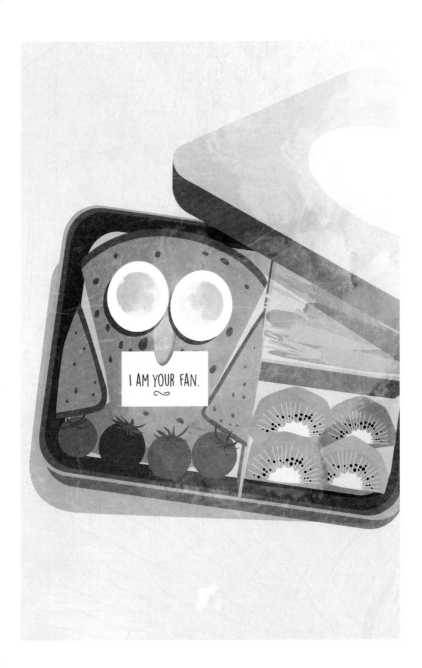

September 21

If you run a business, go the extra mile for your employees by giving everyone the day off on their birthday.

September 22

Organize a bingo or trivia night fund-raiser to help a neighbor in need.

September 23

"Every other week, I take a couple hours out of my schedule to give hand massages and manicures to senior women at a nearby nursing home. I love to see their eyes light up as someone reminds them that they are beautiful inside and out."

September 24

Aim to be early—always—so you don't keep others waiting.

September 25

Rekindle that spark: send your spouse or partner a random text that says, "Love you! Can't wait to see you later!"

September 26

"A few years ago, I helped a neighbor in my community clean up the overgrown land next to her home. She told me that she'd been tidying up the space every year for over 10 years with little help. I eventually organized a group of volunteers to help out each season."

September 27

Do one nice act for yourself each month. Maybe that means treating yourself to a massage, creating a household budget, applying for a new job, or ending a toxic relationship.

September 28

"As a wedding gift, one of my friends gave us $250 in cash along with a note that said, 'This money is not for you. As you travel you will see people who need it. Give some to them. I give you the gift of giving.' As we were on our honeymoon, we saw homeless people who clearly needed help. We doled out the money in 10s and 20s and had some memorable moments because of our friend's kindness."

September 29

Keep your word. It's simple: if you say you're going to do something, do it.

September 30

"My father has a friend who lost her son in a tragic accident just before her wedding. Working with a travel agent, he anonymously paid for her honeymoon, because he wanted her to find some joy in her new life."

October 1

A month before Halloween, collect kids' gently used costumes and donate them to a women and children's shelter.

October 2

"My friend of almost 30 years died of breast cancer, leaving a seven-year-old daughter. Her family couldn't care for her, so I took her into my home. She was going to school 45 miles away, but she liked it there and I wanted her to have some consistency in her life. So I drove 45 miles, twice a day, for seven months, until the school year was over."

October 3

"At my company, we conclude most of our events with a gratitude circle where we stop to take a few moments and sing the praises of others. Even though we are a business, it's always beneficial to share kindness with others."

October 4

Spread your knowledge: if you're a small business owner, mentor someone who's just starting out.

October 5

Call your local children's hospital and ask if there are any kids who are in particular need of a pick-me-up. Swing by with a pile of books and read to them.

October 6

"After I broke my shoulder, several people stepped forward to help, driving me to appointments and helping me with shopping. One friend even replaced the standard seam on some of my T-shirts with Velcro so they would be easy to put on."

October 7

You know those clothes that your infant outgrew in weeks? Pass them along to a new mom.

October 8

The next time you go shopping, pick out a gift for a less fortunate child and donate it to Toys for Tots.

October 9

Knit little booties for newborns and donate them to a hospital pediatric unit.

October 10

At the supermarket, leave a coupon on a grocery store item.

October 11

"We were at the grocery store, and it was One of Those Days. I was at the end of my rope, and the kids were losing their minds. The man bagging our groceries could have been annoyed, but he engaged the kids by being very silly. Then he took our cart to the car and loaded my groceries while I buckled the kids in. It made a difficult trip so much easier."

October 12

"Carry out a random act of seemingly senseless kindness, with no expectation of reward or punishment, safe in the knowledge that one day someone, somewhere, might do the same for you."

— Diana, Princess of Wales

October 13

"The kindergartners at our local elementary school have a particularly fun project: Each student brings in a canned good on our 100th day of school to donate to the local food pantry. Then we all go into the auditorium and count the cans together until we reach 100. The project is called '100 Cans for 100 Days,' and we often surpass our goal."

October 14

"I always try to help parents I see traveling at airports. I know I've appreciated it every time someone offered to entertain my squirmy toddler or hold my baby while I got my bags settled."

October 15

Tape a gas gift card to a gas pump.

October 16

Feel bad that you can't spend time with your friends? Schedule a regular date for a call or video chat, such as the first Sunday of the month at 2 P.M. Then you can connect without all the planning.

October 17

When you go into a doctor's office, or anywhere the staff usually gets more complaints than kind words, bring along a bag of candy to share.

October 18

Write a feel-good letter for a friend who is moving away and give it to her before she leaves with instructions to open it when she's feeling homesick.

October 19

"Last night I ran into an elderly blind gentleman who needed help crossing the street. I ended up walking him a few blocks, arm in arm, to his apartment building. Bonus for me: we had a lovely conversation."

October 20

"A few weeks ago, my family stopped at a crowded restaurant. The only table available was for two. Then a man and his son at a table for four offered to switch with us. It was a small gesture but it meant so much."

October 21

When you go on a trip, bring home a surprise souvenir for a special someone.

October 22

Take the time to sit down and pen a handwritten thank-you note. It's a lost art that is so appreciated.

October 23

Leave your change in a vending machine. Better yet, buy an extra snack or drink for someone to discover.

October 24

Clear out your cupboards and donate what you won't eat to a food pantry. Be sure to check the expiration dates first so the food can actually be eaten.

October 25

"I once witnessed a car accident at a busy intersection. One car ended up on the sidewalk, and the driver had minor injuries. While most of the bystanders, including me, were just staring, one woman approached the car, found the driver's phone, and called his girlfriend to tell her what had happened and what hospital the guy would be taken to."

October 26

Ask your favorite Web-savvy teen to do a tech tutorial with a senior who can't make heads or tails of the Internet.

October 27

Think about two people whose professional skills complement each other and introduce them over dinner at your house.

October 28

Offer to rake leaves for the oldest person on your block.

October 29

"Last week I gave the grocery store clerk and bagger coupons to the movie theater. I had purchased a coupon book from the town lacrosse team. I would never use all the coupons, so I decided to give some away."

October 30

Donate extra vacation days to a co-worker who is struggling with an illness.

October 31

"During the year I buy all sizes of gloves and mittens when they're on sale. Then at Halloween I fill them with candy and give them out to the trick-or-treaters who come to my door. This way they get both treats and something to keep their hands warm."

November 1

"Once our kids are done trick-or-treating, the parents at my son's elementary school collect our extra Halloween candy and ship it overseas to U.S. military families."

November 2

Offer to help an elderly friend move something heavy.

November 3

"My friend recently gave up her seat on an overbooked flight, delaying her flight home an entire day, so that a mother could attend her son's graduation."

November 4

Encourage your local school district to adopt an enrichment program called Choose Love (jesselewischooselove .org), which teaches courage, grati- tude, forgiveness, and compassion in honor of a boy killed in the Sandy Hook shootings.

November 5

"After my baby was born, my husband's grandma would often come over to see us. When the baby went down for a nap, she'd tell me to do the same. I would wake up to find she'd been dusting, doing dishes, folding laundry, and cleaning floors. I miss the days when stuff would get magically done like that!"

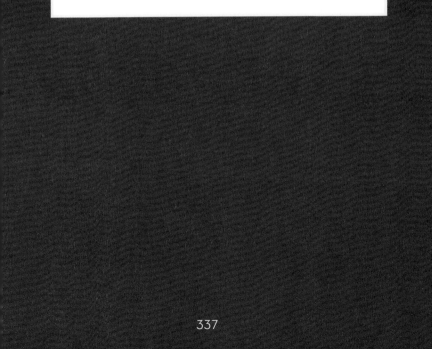

November 6

Offer to drive an elderly neighbor to the polls on Election Day.

November 7

Play board games with a senior citizen at a nursing home.

November 8

Ask guests who come to a holiday party to bring a canned good for a local food pantry instead of a hostess gift.

November 9

Consider donating dolls to seniors who live in a memory care unit. Dementia patients respond well to caring for the "babies."

November 10

"We are the Friday Singers! A group of us performs a 30-minute musical program for rehab patients and residents of retirement homes. We sing the oldies and goodies, accompanied by instruments and choreography. Our audiences love the performances, and we feel blessed to be able to make these visits."

November 11

When you see a member of the armed services in a restaurant (on Veterans Day or any day), thank them for their service and pick up the tab.

November 12

Tap your circle of friends to help others. Organize your book club or mothers' group to take on a community project, such as sprucing up an unused public space or collecting clothes for families in need.

November 13

"Our family was returning home after a trip to Disney World. The security line at the airport was very long, and my husband and I were in despair—our son has disabilities, and crowds and noise overwhelm him. I left my husband standing with him in a corner and ran off to seek help. I caught the eye of a security officer and told her the situation. 'My nephew has autism,' she said. 'I totally get it.' She escorted us through the line, heading off a massive meltdown. This kindness has stayed in my heart ever since."

November 14

"That best portion of a good man's life,
His little, nameless, unremember'd acts
Of kindness and of love."

— William Wordsworth

November 15

"I was parking and had a minor colli-sion with another car. Luckily there was no damage, and the woman in the other car was very understanding. I went inside a nearby supermarket, bought her a gift card, and left it on her wind-shield. I was so grateful that she didn't make a big deal out of the incident."

November 16

Surprise an office buddy with a cup of coffee.

November 17

Pass it on: when someone shows kind-ness to you, set a goal of doing the same within 24 hours.

November 18

"When we take walks, my dog and I visit an elderly neighbor who lives alone."

November 19

Tired of your long hair? Consider cutting it off and donating it to Locks of Love (locksoflove.org), an organization that creates hairpieces for children who have lost their hair to disease.

November 20

Spread luck! Leave pennies heads-side-up on the sidewalk.

November 21

When you're hosting a dinner party or holiday dinner, write something you appreciate about each guest on the back of their place card.

November 22

This month take a few hours to volunteer as a family at a soup kitchen or food pantry.

November 23

As tempting as it may be to jump to conclusions, try hard not to.

November 24

"I had a huge mission event coming up, with well over 100 hours of work left to prepare for the day. My husband had come down with the flu, and I was panicking that I'd get sick too and not be able to finish everything. Not two hours after confessing my fears to a friend from church, she showed up at my door with an immune booster, knowing that I would be tied to my computer for most of the day and wouldn't be able to buy it myself."

November 25

Hold the elevator door for the person dashing in behind you.

November 26

Encourage children to join Kids for Peace (kidsforpeaceglobal.org), which spreads kindness through projects like collecting dollar bills to buy beds in impoverished countries and decorating flip-flops to send to kids in need of shoes.

November 27

Post a picture on social media of you and your best friend—then share why this person is so special to you.

November 28

Offer to organize a friend or loved one's photos for them by putting them into digital albums by year or printing out photo books that mark special occasions like weddings or birthdays.

November 29

"One year I was buying a Christmas tree and the seller told me that the previous customer had paid it forward, so he would give me the tree for free. Instead, I paid it forward again for the next buyer and asked the seller to choose someone who seemed like they needed it."

November 30

Adopt a large senior dog. They are among the least likely to be adopted from a pet shelter.

December 1

During the holidays organize a group of friends to shop for families in need and wrap the gifts. Then deliver the presents in person.

December 2

"This past Christmas we were at a mall, and a woman asked my husband if he would buy her a meal. Without a moment's thought, he said yes, took her to the food court, and had her choose what she wanted. He didn't question her, didn't judge her, just provided what she asked for, because he could."

December 3

Arrange for your child to have a pen pal in another country through ePals .com so he or she can learn about other cultures and traditions.

December 4

"I had on a Christmas necklace, and a woman working at a coat check told me how cute and fun it was. I took it off and handed it to her. Giving it to her made me feel a lot better than wearing it."

December 5

"I broke my leg in December, and while I was in the hospital, my colleagues brought a tree to my house, pulled out my Christmas ornaments, and decorated the tree. I'll never forget their generosity."

December 6

Offer to tutor a student for free in a particular subject area. If you're not confident enough in, say, your foreign language skills, pick a subject you loved in school or use in your work.

December 7

At Christmas, candy cane-bomb a parking lot by placing small candy canes under the wipers on every car.

December 8

"Every year during Advent, our extended family honors my mother, who passed away from breast cancer years ago, with acts of kindness. We document what we do and mail a description of our good deeds to my father, who then reads them aloud after Christmas dinner. We try to guess who each act belongs to."

December 9

When you do your holiday shopping, aim to shop at as many businesses with a mission as you can—or make a donation.

December 10

When you think there's nothing you can do to help in a situation, think again.

December 11

Buy a bouquet of flowers—for yourself.

December 12

"At Christmas I give my grown daughters $50 each and ask them to choose a complete stranger to bless during the holidays. This year one daughter bought gifts for a Christmas Angel Tree and my other daughter gave her money to a girl she encountered who was working three jobs to support her grandmother."

December 13

Get to bring a plus-one to a holiday party? Invite a friend you haven't seen in a while.

December 14

"Send a card or package to armed service members and veterans through a program like the Red Cross's Holidays for Heroes. Consult your regional chapter to see what the biggest needs are in your area."

December 15

"Anytime I pass a holiday bell ringer for charities such as the Salvation Army, I offer to get them a hot chocolate or coffee as well as making a donation."

December 16

"Adopt" a senior at a local senior center and give them a gift during the holidays.

December 17

Make the holidays happen for students who aren't going home for the break: organize friends to cook meals while the dining halls are closed or invite them for a holiday dinner.

December 18

Go caroling around your neighbor-hood with friends to spread holiday cheer. (And throw in some hot mulled cider for your fellow singers when you're done.)

December 19

Hang holiday lights and put up outdoor decorations for neighbors who aren't able to do it themselves.

December 20

Make extra Christmas cookies and package them up to give out to anyone who looks like they might need a sweet treat.

December 21

"Our family left little gifts—candy canes, cards, chocolates—every other day or so for our elderly widowed neighbors across the street for the month of December. It's rough to live alone during the holiday season."

December 22

"One of the biggest kindnesses you can do is to give back to a cause that's deeply personal. As a young teenager, I started at a new high school and knew only a handful of people. The first few months were overwhelming. Then I joined the track team and immediately felt included. So now I love to support Girls on the Run, a nonprofit organization that inspires girls to be joyful, healthy, and confident."

December 23

Looking for a way to involve kids in charitable acts? Check out Kids That Do Good (kidsthatdogood.com), a site that matches children to local age-appropriate volunteer activities.

December 24

A couple in Washington saw a pile of soggy discarded mail on the side of the street. The cards were torn up, so they suspected that thieves had gotten to the envelopes before they were delivered and opened them in search of cash or gift cards. The couple let the mail dry and then hand-delivered every letter to its rightful recipient.

December 25

"On Christmas Day my husband and I went to a pancake house for breakfast. The waitress told us she had asked her young children to wait until she got off work to open their gifts. I felt bad and left her a large tip. We saw her again recently and she remembered us. She told us that she had 'paid it forward' with the money we gave her. During her shift she used the tip money to anony-mously pay the bill for four tables."

December 26

Walking down the sidewalk and need to look at your phone? Step aside and stop. It will keep the pathways clear for everyone else, and you won't cause an awkward collision.

December 27

Record a video of your grandparents or your parents telling their life stories. It's a keepsake that you'll treasure when they're gone.

December 28

"A friend takes old baby blankets and turns them into teddy bears and pillows. It's a lovely memento for moms whose kids are grown."

December 29

When you're at a drive-through, give the attendant an extra $5 to help cover the order for the car behind you.

December 30

Many food pantries accept donations of toiletries in addition to canned goods. Donate toothpaste, shampoo, deodorant, and more. Especially needed are feminine hygiene products and diapers.

December 31

"No act of kindness, no matter how small, is wasted."

— Aesop

About the Author

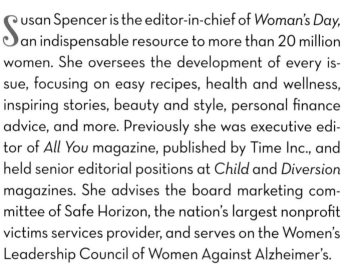

Susan Spencer is the editor-in-chief of *Woman's Day,* an indispensable resource to more than 20 million women. She oversees the development of every issue, focusing on easy recipes, health and wellness, inspiring stories, beauty and style, personal finance advice, and more. Previously she was executive editor of *All You* magazine, published by Time Inc., and held senior editorial positions at *Child* and *Diversion* magazines. She advises the board marketing committee of Safe Horizon, the nation's largest nonprofit victims services provider, and serves on the Women's Leadership Council of Women Against Alzheimer's.

Woman's Day is the #1 selling monthly on U.S. newsstands. The Inspire section is one of the magazine's most widely read, and its centerpiece is the Kindness Project, a column that highlights good deeds and everyday kindnesses done by readers.

We hope you enjoyed this Hay House book. If you'd like to receive our online catalog featuring additional information on Hay House books and products, or if you'd like to find out more about the Hay Foundation, please contact:

Hay House, Inc., P.O. Box 5100, Carlsbad, CA 92018-5100
(760) 431-7695 or (800) 654-5126
(760) 431-6948 (fax) or (800) 650-5115 (fax)
www.hayhouse.com® • www.hayfoundation.org

Published and distributed in Australia by:
Hay House Australia Pty. Ltd., 18/36 Ralph St.,
Alexandria NSW 2015 • Phone: 612-9669-4299
Fax: 612-9669-4144 • www.hayhouse.com.au

Published and distributed in the United Kingdom by:
Hay House UK, Ltd., Astley House, 33 Notting Hill Gate,
London W11 3JQ • Phone: 44-20-3675-2450
Fax: 44-20-3675-2451 • www.hayhouse.co.uk

Published in India by:
Hay House Publishers India, Muskaan Complex, Plot No. 3, B-2,
Vasant Kunj, New Delhi 110 070 • Phone: 91-11- 4176 -1620
Fax: 91-11- 4176 -1630 • www.hayhouse.co.in

Distributed in Canada by:
Raincoast Books, 2440 Viking Way, Richmond, B.C. V6V 1N2
Phone:1-800-663-5714 • Fax: 1-800-565-3770
www.raincoast.com

Access New Knowledge.
Anytime. Anywhere.

Learn and evolve at your own pace
with the world's leading experts.

www.hayhouseU.com